KU-617-687

Matthew Pritchett studied at St Martin's School of Art in London and first saw himself published in the *New Statesman* during one of its rare lapses from high seriousness. He has been the *Daily Telegraph*'s front-page pocket cartoonist since 1988. In 1995, 1996, 1999, 2005, 2009 and 2013 he was the winner of the Cartoon Arts Trust Award and in 1991, 2004 and 2006 he was 'What the Papers Say' Cartoonist of the Year. In 1996, 1998, 2000, 2008 and 2009 he was the *UK Press Gazette* Cartoonist of the Year and in 2015 he was awarded the Journalists' Charity Award. In 2002 he received an MBE.

The Daily Telegraph

30 YEARS OF

ORION

First published in Great Britain in 2018 by Orion Books
A division of the Orion Publishing Group Ltd
Carmelite House
50 Victoria Embankment
London
EC4Y 0DZ

A Hachette UK Company

10 9 8 7 6 5 4 3 2 1

A CIP catalogue record for this book is available from the British Library.

ISBN: 978 1 4091 8098 2

Printed in Italy

www.orionbooks.co.uk

30 YEARS OF

Foreword

by Matt

I really wanted to be a film cameraman. After studying Design and Illustration at St Martin's School of Art I did work experience with the BBC, filming *'Allo 'Allo* in Thetford Forest. After a few months I couldn't afford to keep working for nothing, and I seemed no closer to getting a proper job as a camera assistant, so I decided to bring my not-very-profitable film career to an end. I thought about trying illustration, but I didn't have a portfolio of work to show to anyone. Then I realised if I drew cartoons I wouldn't have to wait to be commissioned, I could just start sending them off. I sent jokes to any magazine I could think of and eventually, after many months, and just before I gave up cartooning as well, one of my jokes appeared in the *New Statesman*. I was so thrilled I went into any newsagent I saw, checking that my cartoon was in each copy of the magazine.

I knew I would go crazy sitting at home on my own trying to think of jokes about desert islands, so I decided to do topical cartoons, which meant the subject for the jokes would change all the time and I could work with other people. And a newsroom isn't so different from a film set, with teams of funny, gossipy people working together – but in an office instead of a forest. In those days the *Telegraph* had a diary called Peterborough, which carried a cartoon every day, and the diary editor would consider any drawing that was dropped off at their Fleet Street office by 3pm. After about six weeks of delivering three cartoons a day, one suddenly appeared, and after a while I was getting in a few every week.

I soon realised if I loitered in the newsroom I'd get asked to do other cartoons when a small hole appeared on a page. Then on 24th February 1988 the *Telegraph* printed the wrong date on the front page; they said it was Thursday 25th a day early. The readers went mad and called in to say they'd had a row in the post office or had gone to a doctor's appointment 24 hours too soon. The editor, Max Hastings, had to write a front page apology and as I was walking through the newsroom someone said to me

'I hope I have a better Thursday than I did yesterday'

'You're a cartoonist, we need something to go with this'. I was so desperate for one of my cartoons to appear on the front page I offered them six different jokes and it worked; one got used – it was the last one I thought of. Within six months I was made the *Telegraph*'s front page cartoonist, but I always think of February 25th as the day it all started.

I'm often asked if jokes just pop into my head at any time, but generally I have to be at my desk in the office. I go in early and start thinking of as many jokes as I can and, after I've had a few ideas, I tend to relax a bit and then ideas that are more original come along. I still show six ideas every day, and I test them out round the office to anyone who'll look at them. By about 4pm I've usually narrowed it down to two or three and the editor picks the final one. I then draw up that one properly and throw all the others in the bin. I worry just as much as I did for my very first front page cartoon and sometimes if I'm not happy with what's been picked, or there's late breaking news, I'll try to think of something new later in the day. I did go back to the office late one evening after a cabinet minister had resigned, but as it gets nearer the 9.30pm deadline for the front page, and people are screaming for the cartoon, it gets much harder to think of something funny.

Sometimes the subjects of my cartoons want the originals which is very flattering. I've done jokes about the royals which they've asked for and a few prime ministers and cabinet ministers have my drawings. A few years ago I was summoned to MI6 to see the head of the British Secret Service at the time, Sir John Scarlett. After going through the most extraordinary levels of security I was shown into his office. He took me over to his desk where there were some of my cartoons. After establishing that I was the Matt who had drawn them (I cracked very easily and confessed straight away) he said 'I want you to do the Christmas card for MI6'. It was one of the great thrills of my life and I still have the thank you note he sent me, written in green ink and signed 'C'.

I think I get my work ethic from my father and grandfather. My father has worked his whole life in newspapers and I've seen how much hard work and anxiety goes into being so consistently funny. My grandfather was a short story writer, literary critic and editor and my sister and I used to visit him in his house near Regent's Park. He would work on the top floor in a little attic room. He had an old pastry board on his lap and he'd write his books longhand on sheets of paper in very spidery writing. And my grandmother would type them up – she was the only person who could read his handwriting. He worked every day, even Christmas Day. It taught me that being creative is just very hard work. But it will do till the BBC gets back to me about that assistant cameraman job.

PS I was very honoured to receive this for my 30th anniversary.

SANDRINGHAM HOUSE

Successful cartoonists do not only need to be able to draw, they have to think of subjects to illustrate. Matt has shown that he has a genius for both, as well as the ability to think of wonderfully appropriate swipes at the idiocies of contemporary life.

'Scientists have discovered a link between not eating your greens and being hit with a saucepan'

Health Scares

'They're the only thing left that is safe to eat'

'How nutty is the cutlet?'

BSE

TYPICAL, AN EMPTY BUS AND THE LOONY SITS NEXT TO ME

BAN ON U.S GROWTH HORMONE BEEF

'Let them eat cake'

BSE

'That's the most impressive case of bird flu I've ever seen'

'Our chef's speciality is chicken cooked in Lemsip'

'I glorified bird flu'

'Wake up. Our duck down duvet just sneezed'

'I only had a bacon sandwich'

'You remember you wanted a pony?'

'What's in this burger? It just jumped over my chips'

Horsemeat scandal

'We are time travellers from the year 2050'

'I think it's fizzy drink o'clock'

Obesity

MATT
NOROVIRUS
ONLY 20 VOMITING DAYS TO CHRISTMAS

Red meat fears

'When I hired you to kill my husband I didn't expect you to come and cook him steak every day'

'Sorry, I now have to wear this every time I sell a packet of cigarettes'

PASSIVE
SMOKING
RISKS

JAMES BOND DECIDES
TO HAVE A CIGARETTE

Smoking

'I never have more than one glass'

'I live in the country and when I'm in London I stay at my drunk tank'

'This is a special occasion, open a can of the 38p lager'

'My alcohol intake? Well, it's a bit early for me, but I'll have a gin and tonic'

'It's important to have two alcohol-free days a week.
We employ a chap in the village to do ours'

Weather

'Look, the Shard'

'You should see the box of fish fingers that got away'

'If you think this is bad you should see Uckfield'

FLOODS

LONDONERS
A BIT TOO
HOT TO
SLEEP

'My husband's too mean to turn up the heating, he just grits the hallway'

'I can't see what's in your eye, but we know it's not grit'

'Our roof was photographed on the A303 doing 85mph'

'We're calling her Imogen because of her terrible wind'

'I filled the duvet with frozen peas'

'It's the perfect crime – I'll water your garden and you can water mine . . .'

Law & Order

'It's a nice day, I think I'll walk back'

'I now declare this juvenile secure unit open'

'Police? Can you see with your High Street video camera if the greengrocer has any broccoli?'

VAN GOGH
MUSEUM
SECURITY
DEPT.

'There was going to be a riot here as well, but we overslept'

'The contenders are: the Police Crime Figures and the NHS Waiting Times'

'It's half-past two, fatty'

'There's a cat stuck up a tree. You can't object on moral grounds'

'It was that one'

'We did it to annoy him'

Military

'A lot of the pageantry has gone since the defence cuts'

'After tank regiments lost their tanks, I have bad news for the Parachute Regiment...'

'I'd shoot myself in the foot if my gun wasn't jammed'

'A delicious contribution to the war effort from the Belgians, eh Sarge?'

'…and I got that one for my bombing raids on Kosovo'

'The British jihadists are the ones wearing socks under their sandals'

Foreign Affairs

'Be careful, they might have pens'

'A second bottle? I think you've expressed enough solidarity with France this evening'

Burqa ban

"You say 'tomaydo', we say 'tomato'. You say 'Trump', we say 'Are you out of your mind?'"

Clinton, Obama and Trump

'I've sold it to Donald Trump'

*'Putin's here.
Everybody ignore him'*

*'We must be nearly back
over the UK; I keep seeing
Russian bombers'*

Russia

'We're the three wise men'

Education

'I don't really mind, but I can't put their paintings on the fridge any more'

'How did sports day go?'

'I'm afraid your car failed the tough new emissions test, but it did get six GCSEs'

'And don't be late tomorrow, it's the school photo . . .'

'He's had a wonderful day'

'I don't know if my phone battery will last that long'

'I wanted to go to the new lesson on responsible sex but I couldn't get a baby-sitter'

'If a triangle has one side of 3cm and another of 4cm, how many private tutors did your parents hire?'

'We've diversified. We're now a pub and grammar school'

'Many of our pupils go on to have successful careers opposing selective schools'

'I shall now attempt to fail a GCSE'

'At least we know you're not taking performance-enhancing drugs'

'It's much harder to fail exams than it was in your day'

'The relentless grade inflation has finally been halted'

'That's not cyber bullying, those are your GCSE results'

'They've made the GCSE results envelope much harder to open'

'How much for just the scarf?'

'Isn't that better than a university degree?'

Sport

'At some time in the next few weeks you're going to see daddy cry...'

'If you don't want to know how your marriage ends, look away now'

'Football has ruined money'

'Here at Liverpool it's the second half – or as Luis Suarez calls it, dessert'

Biting controversy

'It's my husband's birthday, so I'd like to pay for England to win'

'A spot betting syndicate has paid me £150,000 to make a Victoria sponge'

MUIRFIELD
TOILETS
MEN
MEN IN
KILTS

'I wish you'd never heard of Jonny Wilkinson'

Roses are red
Champagne is bubbly
Have a wonderful day
I'll be at the rugby

'And we've just heard that six riders have tested positive for Wensleydale cheese'

'This is what happened when a mosquito bit a Russian athlete'

MATT

'He was watching the showjumping when he fell at the final fence'

'COME ON, whoever you are, keep doing whatever you're doing. YESSS! NO ...have we won?'

London Olympics

Transport

'I rub the balloon on my jumper and the static electricity powers the car'

'Would you take him in part exchange?'

'Are we nearly there yet?'

'Speeding? This isn't my driverless car, it's my wife's driverless car'

'Do we have to pay extra? My husband has a lot of emotional baggage'

'Listen, I've loved spending time with you, but I'm flying back to Gatwick and the chances of us seeing each other again are almost nil . . .'

'And Damien Hirst did the tail fin on this one'

'Could passengers on the lower decks see if we've landed yet'

'I had one holiday romance in Italy and two more in the queue at Heathrow'

'We've found the problem. You're looking at £18 billion plus parts and labour'

Diesel-gate

‘This train has always been called the 8.57, but nobody can remember why’

'Passengers waiting for the 13.22 are advised to use a high factor sun cream'

'Did you have a good day at the railway station, dear?'

*'Day return?
Feeling lucky, sir?'*

'He doesn't play with the trains, he just puts up the fares'

'It's much cheaper if you travel at a different time – the 1950s for example'

'It's to deter binge travelling'

‘My husband’s a Southern Rail driver. He refuses to operate doors’

Politics

'Daddy, why does Tony Blair allow earthquakes to happen?'

'I'm a Liberal Democrat, I'm neither to the left nor to the right'

'It looks like a contest between the Lib Dem big beasts, Thingummy and Whatsisname'

'It's stopped spinning and now it's going on a lecture tour of the US'

'If I had to choose, I'd rather John Prescott punched me . . .'

'Isn't it time you were abolished, dear?'

'Jenkins, go out and kiss some babies for me'

Lords Reform

'Can you tell the fees office I'm designating this as my main residence?'

'As soon as I saw what I'd been up to, I knew the Speaker had to go'

MPs expenses

'Do you think we could fit a plasma TV in there?'

'Be vigilant. I've heard some nutters could be planning a general election'

'I've made a string of promises I can't possibly keep'

'Oh, all right then, take me to Nick Clegg'

Coalition . . .

MATT
10
CLEGG
FLAP

'OH NO! I've left my father running the country!!!'

Cameron leaves daughter in pub

MATT
LIB DEMS
BREAKING
SMALLER PROMISES
THIS TIME

'We'll always have our student loans to remember them by'

'Oh no! Just as I learned to stop calling him Ed – or do I mean David?'

'I DIDN'T vote, I just took a selfie in the booth'

*'I'm studying politics.
The course covers the period
from 8am on Thursday to
lunchtime on Friday'*

Post-Referendum fall-out

'The party is divided. The loonies may split from the fruitcakes'

'My dad's an opinion pollster. I hope he never loses that sense of wonder and surprise at election results'

2017 snap election

'It turns out the voters are bloody difficult as well'

'Hello, I recently bought a strong and stable dining table from you ...'

2017 snap election

The Economy

'This is a hold-up. Move slowly towards the till and buy something'

'I'm afraid I'm going to have to ask you to leave'

'It's a marvel of evolution – an out-of-worker bee'

'No pension, no mortgage, no shares – suddenly I'm a financial genius'

MATT
CHRISTMAS CREDIT CRUNCH
FRANKIN-
CENSE
MYRHH
SOCKS

'There are no tea bags left. We're staring into the abyss'

'Welcome to the store. Are you returning something or have you just come in to use the loo?'

'To be honest I just follow the rest of the market'

'Mr Darling isn't here. It looks like he's making a statement at the moment'

'. . . About your nest egg – I've made you an omelette'

'Listen, men. Stealing from the poor hasn't been as popular as I'd hoped . . .'

'GONE BUST? Is that the tour operator or the country?'

'I went for a dip this morning. A double dip is now a possibility'

'I remember when you could buy a pint, have a haircut and go to the cinema for exactly what it costs now'

'Some time ago I lent you my ladder. You now owe me 236 ladders'

Banks

'They didn't have any money'

'I'm a banker. Would you give my bill to one of the other tables'

'Just give us your ******* money'

'I'm a taxpayer. How would you like the money – twenties or fifties?'

'The politicians promised us that only our children would suffer'

'That's the riskier side of the bank'

'I can't give you a bonus but there's a £2m reward for the person who finds my umbrella'

'I didn't realise numbers went this small'

'Will sir be lining his own pockets?'

House Prices

'We'll never get a taxi. Let's just buy one of these houses'

'Your pocket money is for sweets – you weren't meant to buy a house'

'How much is this house? ....And how much is it now?'

'As you can see, this property has spectacular views of the recession'

'Fortunately, the food price inflation cancels out the fall in house prices'

'For goodness sake, man!
House prices aren't a suitable topic for dinner parties'

'It's one of the earliest examples of builders flouting local planning laws'

'Have you seen the neighbours' new extension?'

'This looks like a nice spot'

'And this one has uninterrupted views over Kent'

'The defence cuts have freed up these magnificent starter homes'

'We're first time buyers and the Government helped us get this pothole'

MATT

HOUSE PRICE BOOM

FOR SALE

'We'll take it'

'My husband opened our gas bill and exploded'

Energy

'This is a hold-up.
Fill this balloon with gas'

'That reminds me, it must be
time to bleed the customers'

*'I don't have a complaint.
I'm just here because it's so lovely and warm'*

'Do you have any candles that can charge an iPhone?'

'We're fracking for worms'

'Faster! The lights are dimming'

Europe

'I doubt if we'll see European monetary union in our lifetime'

'If I hadn't got out a copy of the Maastricht treaty they would never have left'

MATT

GREEK CALENDAR
CRUNCH DAY
LAST CHANCE
11th HOUR
THIS IS IT
MAKE or BREAK
END-GAME
D-DAY
JUDGMENT DAY
THE BRINK

'It's no longer "if" I have another ouzo, it's "when"'

Greek crisis

Brexit

'We can't BLAME Europe if we're not IN Europe'

'Don't leave. You'll be poorer, have less influence and it might lead to war in Europe'

'We don't need to be part of a failing EU, we're big enough to fail on our own'

'Let's never ask the public for their views ever again'

Leave wins

‘If the UK is destroyed in a nuclear attack, these are the codes for triggering Article 50’

'Mary Berry will now tell us how to prevent our hard Brexit having a soggy bottom'

'It's an EU themed restaurant. We don't tell them what we want and they don't give it to us'

'Two Englishmen in Whitehall. One says "Which way to Brexit?" The other one replies "I wouldn't start from here"'

'If they offer us coffee, hold out for the biscuits as well'

Migration

'I think I've invented the migrant crisis'

'I voted UKIP. Well, to be honest, I paid a Bulgarian to go and do it for me'

'Come to the front of the queue if you can play cricket'

'Ready? The first to 21 points gets into the country'

'I suddenly feel terribly depressed about the cricket'

'I want to impress Theresa May, so I'm going to stop her coming back into the country'

Health

'There are four seasons: Winter NHS crisis, Spring NHS crisis, Summer NHS crisis and Autumn NHS crisis'

'After knocking the Health Secretary to the floor, put your hands round his throat . . .'

'When you said my husband would be a guinea pig . . .'

'Give it to me straight, Doc, how long will my car have to spend in the hospital car park?'

'And when the music stops ...'

'The doctor's on strike, so I had his stitches done by the vet'

'Wrong leg? Apart from that, would you describe yourself as completely satisfied?'

'Ooh, that looks nasty. I'll get someone to kiss it better'

Farming & Fishing

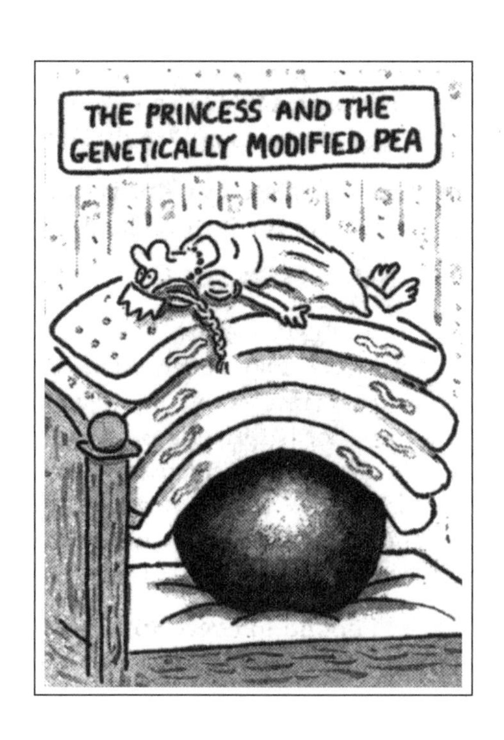

'They've got subsidy blight'

'IT LIVES!!!'

'We shouldn't get sentimental about them; they carry so much disease'

'Every time I seek medical advice online, it recommends shooting or gassing'

'Cheer up, mate, there are plenty more fish in the . . . well, cheer up anyway'

Retirement

'. . . and the smaller pensioners could go up chimneys . . .'

'A few nice days and then it's all over — that's my pension, not the summer'

'Your pension will be fine as long as you don't do anything rash like retire'

'The grandchildren are here.
You distract them while I steal their pocket money'

'The retirement home is full, but if you stop paying your council tax there's a good local prison'

MATT
RETIREMENT MAY BE
FURTHER AWAY THAN
IT APPEARS IN MIRROR

'What do we want? Why did we come here? What were we saying?'

The Royals

'Nice card from Prince Philip'

'There are three of us in this cinema'

Fergie and Diana

QUEEN'S RECORD-
BREAKING REIGN

Prince Philip retires

Religion

'The vicar's trying to compete with the Sunday-opening supermarkets'

'I'm against female bishops, I believe a woman's place is on the front line'

'It's a woman bishop, it can move any way it wants'

Modern Life

'WAIT!...I can make RoboDog wave goodbye'

'Darling, am I in favour of self rule?'

'I know you're excited, but the sooner you go to sleep, the sooner it will be bin day'

'This tall dark stranger – will he be emptying my dustbin?'

*'It will be two weeks before I can see you again,
but I do see some people privately'*

'And now my male colleague will read the Autocue more expensively'

'You can always tell the females – they have the smaller salaries'

'Maybe it will be a bishop or a Cabinet Minister, or perhaps it's just a boy'

'Sometimes I feel like I'm a man trapped inside a woman's salary'

'Stay still! I think you've got the God particle in your eye'

'Something has to be done about these size-zero whippets'

'I'm on the Atkins diet – I don't know if I'm allowed coconuts'

'My name is Rex and I chase foxes'

'We're going to have to shoot the staff'

'Go away! I'm watching the Bake Off final'

'Bad news, we've only got one half of the double entendres'

MATT
Dr WHO
50th ANNIVERSARY

'You've got radical cleric mice. They're impossible to get rid of'

'Let's be frank: If we're going back to your place,
should I buy some fruit and veg?'

'If I don't have it on a chain round my neck I forget where I left it'

'I was 35 when I decided I didn't want to have children, but it was too late'

'He brought opera to the masses – I'll never forgive him for that'

'I had no idea the Duke of Westminster owned all this as well'

MATT
WAR H RSE

'So there's a chance you won't be getting so many home shopping catalogues?'

'We have this huge backlog of "Sorry You Were Out" cards to deliver'

'WE'VE FLOWN INTO AN iCLOUD'

'Someone has leaked a nude oil painting of our déjeuner sur l'herbe'

Celebrities hacked

'If anyone asks, I was with you last night'

'What on earth are you doing? Do you realise how much a TV Licence costs?'

‘A lottery ticket and, to hell with the odds, I’ll have a first class stamp as well’

'I was just ringing to say my test is going brilliantly'

'This is so much better than sniffing each other's bottoms'

'Before the cat got its passport it was always bringing us back dead birds'

'Let's invite your family for Christmas'

'He just melted – nobody shot him'

MATT

SAVE DARTS
PETITION

Pete
Olly
JIM
John
Roger
Ian
Steve
Tony
Nick
Fred
Dave

'We were hoping you were going to sing'

'Apparently, by 2010 you'll be obese and I'll be Polish'

'It's pretty good, but you're no Adolf Hitler'

Painting by Hitler sold

'He's captured brilliantly the lack of facilities, transport and cheap housing in rural areas'

'Scratch away the surface to reveal three Cezannes and win £50,000'

'I'M ON THE TRAIN'

'My password has been hacked.
A cyber-jihadi group now knows the names of our pets'

MATT

WORLD'S FIRST 'SELFIE'

'I heard an oil tanker's run aground. I wonder if it's us'

'And this little piggy grew a pancreas for human transplant'

'Don't kiss it better. I want you to refer me to a personal injury lawyer'

'I attend as many parenting classes as I can –
anything to get away from my children'

IRA STILL
HAS
WEAPONS

'Have you finished with the Wellbeing survey?'

'I see you asked the man who cuts our hedge to give you a receipt'

'How much anti-wrinkle cream did you use?'

'We've been married for 34 years. It was a sham wedding that went wrong'

'I'm so depressed. I've been eating only veg and I'm back up to 65 tons'

'They don't check our internet history, do they?'

MATT
NASA FINDS WATER
MAN WALKS ON MARS– GETS VERRUCA

'On second thoughts, could I have my brick back?'

'A customer has sent us a complaint about our broadband service'

'I am just going online. I may be some time'

'Our electricity comes from a Chinese power station.
If we mention the Dalai Lama the lights go out'

'We got it for its pouch. We save a fortune on plastic carrier bags'

'I've told you before – no Samsung phones at the dinner table'

'You borrowed Daddy's phone. Try to remember where you moved my bank account to'

'The souvenir tea towels are coming 20 minutes apart'

'I had a sex robot, but it ran off with the fridge'

MATT
VET
2.30P
DIGNITAS
2.30pm